ESQUIVEL!

Susan Wood

ILLUSTRATED BY

Duncan Tonatiuh

SPACE-AGE SOUND ARTIST

Charlesbridge

When Juan García Esquivel was a small boy, he lived with his family in Tampico, Mexico, where whirling mariachi bands let out joyful yells as they stamped and strummed.

RINTY-TIN-TIN!

By age six, Juan was curious about music. There was a piano at Juan's house, but it was a player piano—a paper roll told it which keys to play. Clever Juan had an idea. He disabled the paper roll and turned his parents' jangly piano into one he could practice on. He played it day and night.

By age ten, Juan was captivated by music. He loved to play piano—anytime, anywhere. Sometimes he'd disappear from home in search of an audience, and his family would have to go looking for him. They always found him in front of a piano.

When Juan's family moved to Mexico City, the country's bustling capital,
Juan found work playing piano at Mexico's first twenty-four-hour radio station.
He performed for fifteen minutes each day and was paid two pesos a show—
enough to buy a sandwich and a taxi ride home. He was just fourteen years old.

Juan started learning all he could on his own—no music teachers, lessons, or schools. Without traditional training in how musical notes went together, Juan focused instead on how sounds could be arranged. Finally, Juan felt ready to create his own music. So when at age seventeen he was offered the job of orchestra leader for a popular comedy show at the radio station, Juan gladly took it.

When the radio comedian needed music for a skit about, say, a stout man walking his tiny poodle down a busy city street, Juan had to imagine what that might sound like.

Juan might ask the kettle drums to BOWM-BOWM! BOWM-BOWM! like a lumbering giant.

He might ask the clarinets and oboes to YIP! and YAP! like a dainty dog.

He might tell the trumpets and trombones to HONK! BLAP! BLEEP! like blaring car horns.

ZOWWWW

Juan tested and mixed and blended and arranged all sorts of sounds to match the imaginary situation. He was an artist, using dips and dabs of color to create a vivid landscape. But instead of paint, Juan used sound. Weird and wild sounds! Strange and exciting sounds!

Juan started experimenting with popular Mexican tunes. He tinkered with tempos, slowing songs down, then revving them up. He fiddled with dynamics, swapping soothing soft sounds and startling loud sounds. He twisted chords and combined instruments to sound thrilling, dreamy, and often funny, because Juan liked music that made people laugh. But underneath the humor, it took great musical skill to play Juan's challenging new music.

ZINN NEEEE

Nobody had ever heard music like Juan's. Soon he was winning awards. His songs were turned into records that people could buy in stores. Juan's innovative music could be heard on radios and record players all across Mexico.

An important record company in the United States heard about Juan and his unusual music. Would he come make records in America? Yes! Yes! Yes!

¡Sí! ¡Sí! ¡Sí!

Juan packed two suits. He bought a big red convertible sports car with a white top. Then he drove all the way to New York City.

VROOOOOM!

There Juan found a music shop the size of a department store,
with three entire floors full of strange and exotic instruments.

He saw
BOOBAMS,
bamboo tubes that
could play a tune,

BUMPA
BOODA

DUMPA
BUM!

a spooky-sounding electrical
instrument called a
THEREMIN,

OEEEEOOOoo

Bzzz!
Bzzz!

a **BUZZIMBA**, a kazoo-
sounding contraption played
with a mallet,

the **ONDIOLINE**, an organ with a swaying keyboard,

NEE NEE-EE-AH! NEE-EE-AH!

and even a giant **GONG**.

BONGGGGGG 'ggggg

So many odd, new sounds to play with—Juan was in heaven!

The late 1950s and early 1960s was a great time to be recording music. Scientists had discovered a new process called stereophonics, or "stereo" for short. It separated sounds so when you listened to a recording, music could seem to come from the left side, the right side, or both sides at once. For sound artist Juan, stereo was yet another exciting color for his musical palette.

stereo: the sound your eyes can follow

To make a good stereo recording, instruments needed to be kept apart while they were recorded. That way, the **BRAP!** of the horns wouldn't get mixed in with the **WHEEDY-WHEE!** of the flutes. Most conductors used curtains, screens, or special booths to separate the instruments. That wasn't enough for Juan. Once he put half his orchestra in one recording studio and the other half . . .

. . . in another recording studio on the other side of the building—so far it felt
like they were an entire city block away! The musicians wore earphones so they
could hear what they were playing. And so that everyone could see him, Juan
conducted on closed-circuit TV, television only the musicians could view.

Juan had one more sonic trick up his sleeve. He brought in singers. But the singers didn't sing words—they sang sounds. They'd sing "ZU-ZU-ZU!" and "DOO!" and "POW!"

PA-BA-BA-BA-BA!
Roo-Roo-Roo!

On Juan's quirky versions of popular songs, he'd replace the lyrics everyone knew with the singers' fun, flashy sounds.

People loved Juan's colorful music. It took them to other worlds, other planets. It sounded like a crazy rocket ride zigzagging through outer space!

When Juan wasn't making his unique music, he enjoyed many things. He liked beautiful art, fancy cars, and elegant clothes. He especially liked pretty women. But Juan loved music most.

In Las Vegas, Juan and his musicians performed at the Stardust Hotel for fourteen years in a row. Fans from near and far—including famous singers, actors, and actresses—would come to hear his out-of-this-world sounds. Juan also made music for dozens of movies and television programs— even a TV show especially for children.

BRAVO! ENCORE!

Now Juan wasn't called Juan anymore. He'd explored sonic frontiers, expanded musical possibilities, and enhanced the way people think about, listen to, and enjoy music. Now Juan was the space-age sound artist known simply as **ESQUIVEL!**—with an exclamation point!

AUTHOR'S NOTE

I first heard Esquivel's out-of-this-world music in the early 1990s, when I was a journalist writing about popular music for newspapers and magazines. Young people in big cities such as New York, Los Angeles, and Chicago were bored with what they heard on the radio and went digging through their parents' old record collections for interesting music. Esquivel quickly became one of their favorite artists. Record companies reissued CDs of the albums Esquivel had recorded on vinyl three decades earlier. These CDs sold thousands of copies and introduced a whole new generation—including me—to Esquivel's wildly imaginative music.

No one was more astonished by his newfound popularity than Esquivel. He hadn't recorded an album in many years, having shifted his focus to composing for film and television, including the Mexican children's program *Odisea Burbujas*. "I was very surprised," he said in 1995. "I made the recordings quite a long time ago, so it was the past for me. . . . I never did think some people might be interested in my recordings."

The fresh interest in Esquivel was part of a larger trend of rediscovering lounge music. Lounge music is a contemporary term for a type of easy-to-listen-to music that was popular in the 1950s and 1960s. The music seemed to transport listeners to another place—a tropical island, a jungle, or outer space. It had roots in jazz and often folded in exotic sounds—rhythms, melodies, instruments, even animal calls—from faraway places. The music was relaxing—you could lounge around listening to it. In the late 1980s and 1990s, new artists began experimenting with the older lounge-music style and put their own creative spin on the sound.

As many people do, when I listen to Esquivel's quirky compositions, I see pictures in my head. His music suggests all sorts of places, creatures, and activities—with sound. In 1961 a comedian named Ernie Kovacs imagined a whole office and kitchen full of gadgets, furniture, appliances—and even a roast chicken—dancing to Esquivel's songs. Innovative short films, made by manipulating items via remote control, aired nationwide on Kovacs's TV specials. Though Esquivel died in 2002, he's an inspiration to artists in many fields—from musicians to animators to filmmakers—who appreciate his originality and imagination. One group of musicians enjoys Esquivel's music so much that they formed a twenty-two-piece orchestra to play only Esquivel's work. This big band, called Mr. Ho's Orchestrotica, is based in Boston, Massachusetts, and brings Esquivel's brilliant music to audiences around the world, including those in his homeland, Mexico.

Esquivel also left a legacy as a pioneer of stereo sound, now used just about everywhere, such as in surround-sound TV and movies and stereo CDs, MP3s, and other aural media. Esquivel's cultural significance was honored in 2010 when his classic composition "Mini Skirt" was featured prominently in "Yo México," an arena show commemorating the centennial of the Mexican Revolution. Almost a million people attended the four-day multimedia spectacular in Mexico City. Esquivel would surely have been proud to be part of it.

While researching this book, I read many interviews with Esquivel. One of my favorite stories that he tells is about a Chicago newspaper columnist unfamiliar with his music and the exclamation point that accompanied his name. "Before we opened," Esquivel recalled, "he wrote in his column, 'Esquivel! Why?' He came to the show, and I showed him why. . . . The next week in his column, he wrote, 'Esquivel is so good, he deserves two exclamation points.'"

I couldn't agree more!!

ILLUSTRATOR'S NOTE

I had a lot of fun illustrating this book. I wasn't familiar with Esquivel's music, so I enjoyed listening to his songs for the first time and learning about his life. I tried to capture some of the energy and humor of Esquivel's music in my drawings. This project was also a great opportunity to experiment with hand-written type and to study fashion from Esquivel's time.

Esquivel sometimes used traditional Mexican songs, such as "Bésame Mucho" or "La Bamba," in his music and reworked them to add his own particular flavor. He slowed parts down, sped other parts up, and incorporated unusual instruments and original sounds. He breathed new life into traditional songs and made them fun and interesting to new generations of listeners.

I try to do something similar to that with my illustrations. My images are inspired by ancient Mexican art, especially the Mixtec codex of the fourteenth and fifteenth centuries. Like the people and animals in the codex, the figures in my illustrations are always drawn in profile—their entire bodies are usually shown, and their ears often look like a number three. I also collage textures and photographic elements into my images electronically, using special computer software. I hope that like Esquivel, I, too, am breathing new life into a tradition of art, making books fun and interesting to young readers.

Mixtec codex (Zouche-Nuttall). Copyright © The Trustees of the British Museum.

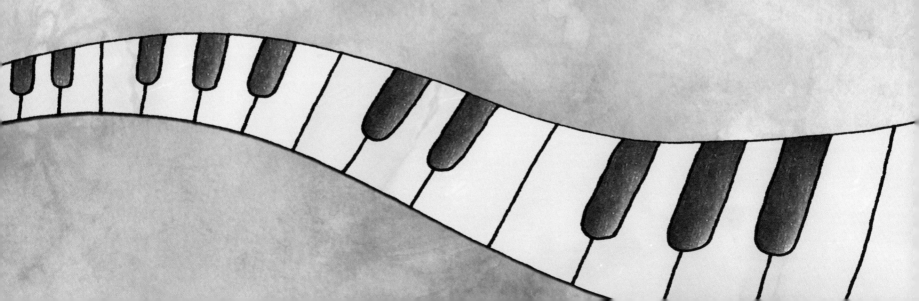

Resources

Source Notes for the Author's Note

"I was very surprised . . . in my recordings": Morgenstern, p. 142.

"Before we opened . . . exclamation points": Thomas Conner, "Is It Live or Is It Esquivel?" *Chicago Sun-Times*, October 2, 2005.

Books and Periodicals

Morgenstern, Hans. "Esquivel: Other Worlds, Other Sounds." *Goldmine Magazine*, October 13, 1995, 81–84, 142, 183.

Vale, V. "Juan García Esquivel." In *Re/Search #15: Incredibly Strange Music*, vol. 2, edited by V. Vale and Andrea Juno, 150–167. San Francisco: Re/Search Publications, 1994.

Web Pages and Websites

The websites and video links listed below were current at the time of publication. To find out more about Esquivel, try searching for his name using your favorite search engine.

Learn about Esquivel's role in developing stereo sound.
Kaliss, Jeff. "Soundtrack for Modern Living: Esquivel in Orbit." Eichler Network website.
http://www.eichlernetwork.com/article/soundtrack-modern-living-esquivel-orbit

Learn more about Esquivel's life and work and listen to samples of his music.
Holmes, Joseph. "Esquivel!" Space Age Bachelor Pad Music website.
http://www.josephholmes.io/spaceage/esquivel/esquivel.html

Read a 1996 interview with Esquivel.
Molenda, Michael. "Space Age Pioneer." Electronic Musician, September 15, 2006.
http://www.emusician.com/artists/1333/space-age-pioneer/37034

Listen to music clips and watch videos of the world's only Esquivel tribute band.
Mr. Ho's Orchestrotica website. http://orchestrotica.com

Video

Watch Ernie Kovacs's films, featuring gadgets, appliances, furniture, and more "dancing" to Esquivel's music.
Kitchen Symphony.
https://www.youtube.com/watch?v=16yl-uQqcFA
Musical Office.
https://www.youtube.com/watch?v=4EXKMJ4LMKA

See a portion of the "Yo México" celebration featuring Esquivel's "Mini Skirt."
https://www.youtube.com/watch?v=co4sE4T7PSE

Watch an interview with Juan García Esquivel, circa 1968.
https://www.youtube.com/watch?v=rqdLrEA4uQQ

Courtesy of Carina Osorio Perez and Irwin Chusid

For aspiring sound artists everywhere—S. W.

To my brother and those who dance even when
others don't hear the music—D. T.

A special thanks to Irwin Chusid, Brother Cleve, Arturo Jímenez,
Glen Morrow, and Brian O'Neill for their expert comments and
feedback on the manuscript and art.

Text copyright © 2016 by Susan Wood
Illustrations copyright © 2016 by Duncan Tonatiuh
All rights reserved, including the right of reproduction in whole or in part in any form. Charlesbridge
and colophon are registered trademarks of Charlesbridge Publishing, Inc.

Published by Charlesbridge
85 Main Street
Watertown, MA 02472
(617) 926-0329
www.charlesbridge.com

Library of Congress Cataloging-in-Publication Data
Names: Wood, Susan, 1965— | Tonatiuh, Duncan, illustrator.
Title: Esquivell: space-age sound artist/Susan Wood; illustrated by Duncan Tonatiuh.
Description: Watertown, MA: Charlesbridge, [2016]
Identifiers: LCCN 2015026827 | ISBN 9781580896733 (reinforced for library use) | ISBN 9781607348252
(ebook) | ISBN 9781607348269 (ebook pdf)
Subjects: LCSH: Esquivel, Juan Garcia—Juvenile literature. | Composers—Mexico—Juvenile literature.
Classification: LCC ML3930.E83 V36 2016 | DDC 780.92—dc23 LC record available at
http://lccn.loc.gov/2015026827

Printed in China
(hc) 10 9 8 7 6 5 4 3 2 1

Illustrations hand-drawn, then collaged digitally
Display type set in Swung Note, designed by PintassilgoPrints
Text type set in Helenita by Rodrigo Typo
Color separations by Colourscan Print Co Pte Ltd, Singapore
Printed by 1010 Printing International Limited in Huizhou, Guangdong, China
Production supervision by Brian G. Walker
Designed by Susan Mallory Sherman